TEMPERED EDGES

A
RECLAMATION

C.B. MOTTOR

Chapbook I

ISBN: 979-8-9935682-0-1

Though the following material is inspired by the poet's lived experiences, any similarities or likeness to any individual, living or deceased, are coincidental.

Photography by C.B. Mottor.
Book design by Shadow Dog Press in-house artists.
Cover Art by C.B. Mottor, in collaboration with Shadow Dog Press in-house Artists. Graphics are licensed through Canva Pro.

First edition 2026.

Shadow Dog Press
North Adams, MA 01247
ShadowDogPress.com

To all the 'me's I was before—
we're going to be okay.

To those
still *out with lanterns.*

And to my mother—You deserve far
more than this world has given you. I
am proud to be *'my mother's daughter.'*

CHAPBOOK CONTENTS

BUTCHER, ME

I cleave myself
into pieces,
fresh to order
for your comfort—

Please, take a number.

Too provocative
to be substantial
but too substantial
to provoke,
so I package
my portions
in neat little boxes
bound tight with
pretty pink bows,
shaving off slivers
soft sensibilities
deem shocking,
carving out chunks
found too sinewed and gnarled—

Here is your pound of flesh
perfectly trimmed
to suit your tastes...

I AM MY MOTHER'S DAUGHTER

"Do as I say, not as I do,"
She always said,
but I waded through
Mascara Rivers and
clamored over the bodies
of her Fallen Lovers
only to spawn
torrents and wreak
carnage of my own.
Childhood Memories
still hold the scent
of Peach Schnapps
and Popov Perfume.

WORTH

*Am I
not worth
my weight
in gold?
In shit?
In soot or sand?
Don't I deserve
the kind touch
of a gentle hand?
A second thought?
A safe place to land?
Have I not earned
the space where I stand?
Room to speak my truth?
Only to supply the demand?
To smooth out all my kinks
so they don't ruin your plans?
I'm not even worth your time
if I don't follow commands?
After all this,
finally now,
I understand
I will never
be enough,
not ever
just
as
I am.*

THE PEELING

You have a beautiful smile.

It's so interesting that you write.

Tell me your thoughts.

Your laugh is infectious.

I love your little quirks.

But not that one.

What are you smiling about?

Don't think like that.

Don't touch your face.

Stand up straight.

Don't write about that.

Uncross your arms.

No, not like that.

Don't laugh so loud.

I said stop touching your face.

Don't talk with your hands.

UNCROSS YOUR FUCKING ARMS!

How many times have I told you?

Don't stand like that.

Stop talking.

Don't walk away from me.

Look at me when I'm talking to you.

Stop, where do you think you're going?

Come back.

Why are you leaving?

You could have been perfect.

PRETTY POISON

I know,
you wanted
a prize-winning
rose in bloom,
not this dandelion
growing from the crack
in your walkway.

Someday you'll learn
pretty petals
laced with pesticides
don't compare
to healing brews
and granted wishes.

MIS(S)FIT

A Failed Madonna
demoted to Whore
A pawn just for you
to hate or adore

Desensitized and disillusioned
through systematic collusion,
I detest your condescension
and reject societal intentions.

I have no affections
left for proffer
There is no treasure
in this coffer

So cease your toil,
this is stark
and barren soil.

Cull the notion
of seeding love
and cultivating
obedient devotion

There is no depth
to inbox transgressions
sown with erotic aggressions—
The burden of your obsessions
distorts My Singularity—
I am NOT your Trophy!
Don't come menace me
with your binds of
monogamistic atrophy.

My "No." is not a challenge
to conquer with romantic incessance
you're a grinding wheel against My Nature
attempting to contort My Essence
But *These Tempered Edges*
Will Not. Be. Worn.

Such Loathsome impositions—
your Gendered Expectations
I'm declaring My Disdain
for domestic obligation,
patriarchal postulation,
and feminine subjugation

Retract your projections—
All your emotional intentions

This heathen is godless—
I am not your Goddess
No shackled Aphrodite
to massage your injured psyche
I'd sooner be The Succubus
insatiable and covetous
Now light the torch
and start the blaze
Avert your eyes—

I Am
Medusa's Gaze

BALLAD

Mama told her
she could always come home
but Mama's there dealing
with a hell of her own

So she writes in the nighttime
putting words on the page
She talks of her sadness
and she talks of her rage

She shares all her dreams
and she shares all her hopes
about why she stopped praying
to the holy ghost

Every word read
is a cent in the bank
Writing down her feelings
Gonna fund her escape.

FAÇADE

She picked a pink farmhouse
out on Mohawk Trail
with a painted picket fence
for their little love tale
but the mask started slipping
as the years rolled by
now her heart is slowly dying
from the insults and fights
There's rats in the garden
and the paint won't dry
so she crept out the door
in the dead of the night
she drove down the trail
and her soul felt right
when that pink farmhouse
was gone from her sight.

FOR THE
RECORD

I don't need your shoulder—

I have these words,
on this page—

Untwisted and Indelible.

LIVING SIN

I'm not supposed to be here.
This bastard soul within
slipped the gates of The Guf—
became my mother's living sin.

Living in a hurry
each breath is stolen time,
like admission was a quarter
but I only paid a dime.

One can't best a vengeful god
and not expect ill fate,
so I revel in this flesh and bone
until my judgment date.

PHOENIX

Chin up,
Darling one,
turn your face
up to the sun.

The day is here,
the time is now.
Find the strength
somewhere,
somehow.

Burn the Bridges.

    Bury the Bodies.

        Wash your face.

            Adjust that Crown.

Today, you rise again.

C.B. Mottor

C.B. Mottor pens raw and evocative poetry and prose driven by lived experience and shaped by chronic illness, mental health struggles, love, loss, and life-altering traumas.

Apart from her writing, she shares artistic photography focused on finding beauty in the chaos, celebrating the skin we're in, and exploring what it means to be a perfectly imperfect, deeply flawed, yet hopeful human being.

C is proud to be the founder and EIC of Shadow Dog Press and The SDL Review antholo-journal.

When she isn't creating, you can find her in her cottage garden with a cup of coffee and Leia, the elder cat, or out hiking with her dogs, Shadow and Padmé, in the Berkshires and beyond.

SPECIAL THANKS
to my friends

James,
Stu,
Journey Bleau,
Jim & The Wizbangs,
Dr. Steve,
Ernie,
Dan,
Spirits of Idaho,
and Cleggy.

C. B. MOTTOR TITLES

FROM

SHADOW DOG PRESS

CHAPBOOK I

TEMPERED EDGES
A RECLAMATION
OUT NOW

CHAPBOOK II

NEEDS INTERTWINED:
THE TANGLED AND TWISTED KIND
COMING FEBRUARY 2026

CHAPBOOK III

SA DANSE MACABRE
RELEASE TBA

-AND-

COLLECTED:
THE COMPLETE WORKS
OF C.B. MOTTOR
(WORKING TITLE)
RELEASE TBA

www.ingramcontent.com/pod-product-compliance
Lightning Source LLC
Chambersburg PA
CBHW071228130626
46555CB00004B/1894